FIRST COMMUNION CATECHISM

Instructions for First Confession and Communion

By
REV. LAWRENCE G. LOVASIK, S.V.D.
Divine Word Missionary

According to the
National Catechetical Directory

CATHOLIC BOOK PUBLISHING CORP.
NEW YORK

This Edition is Dedicated to
SAINT JOSEPH
the Foster Father of JESUS
Husband of the VIRGIN MARY
Protector of the CATHOLIC CHURCH

NIHIL OBSTAT: Michael J. Wren, M.A., M.S.
Censor Librorum

IMPRIMATUR: James P. Mahoney, D.D.
Vicar General, Archdiocese of New York

Name . . . .

School . . . .

I was born on . . . .

I was born again in Baptism on . . . .

(T-250)
ISBN 978-0-89942-250-3
© 1984 Catholic Book Publishing Corp., N.Y.
Printed in China
www.catholicbookpublishing.com

CPSIA October 2016 10 9 8 7 6 5 4 3 2 1 S/D

CONTENTS

Part Nine — THE MORAL LIFE

Part Ten — MARY AND THE SAINTS

Part Eleven — UNION WITH GOD IN HEAVEN

Appendices

The Holy Trinity — three Persons in one God

Part One — GOD

1 THE HOLY TRINITY

1. What does the history of salvation tell us?
The history of salvation tells us
how God saved us.

2. How do we know about God?
We know about God
because he made himself known to us.

3. How did God make himself known to us?
God made himself known to us
through his holy Word in the Bible.

4. What is the Bible?
The Bible is the written story of God's
actions in the world.

5

5. What are the Gospels?

The Gospels are the written story
which tells us
about the words and actions
of Jesus Christ.

6. What did Jesus tell us about God?

Jesus taught us that in the one God
there are three Persons,
Father, Son, and Holy Spirit.

7. What is the mystery of the Holy Trinity?

The mystery of the Holy Trinity
is the one true God in three Persons
—the Father, the Son, and the Holy Spirit.

8. What did Jesus teach us about the Father?

Jesus taught us to love
our heavenly Father
because he loves us
and wants to help us,
and to bring us to his heavenly home.

9. What did Jesus teach us about himself?

Jesus taught us that he is the Son of God
who became man to save us.

10. What did Jesus teach us about the Holy Spirit?

Jesus taught us that the Holy Spirit
is the third Person of the Blessed Trinity,
whom the Father and he sent
to his Church.

11. How do we honor the Blessed Trinity?

We honor the Blessed Trinity
when we pray to God—
the Father, the Son, and the Holy Spirit—
who lives in our soul by grace.

Glory be to the Father and to the Son and to the Holy Spirit

Jesus in the Mass — Our greatest gift to God.

2   WORSHIP OF GOD

12. How has God shown his love for us?

God has shown his love for us
by making us that we may serve him;
by sending his Son to save us from sin;
by loving and caring for us as a loving
Father.

13. How do we show our love for God?

We show our love for God by worshiping
him.

14. How do we worship God?

We worship God by doing
all that he wants us to do;
by praying to him;
by offering ourselves to him
through Jesus in the Mass.

15. Why do we worship God especially in Holy Mass?

We worship God especially in Holy Mass
because in Holy Mass Jesus offers himself
to his Father,
as he did on the cross,
but he does not suffer anymore.
He gives God the highest honor.

16. Why did God put us in this world?

God put us in this world
to know and love him;
to serve him
by keeping his commandments;
to get ourselves ready
for the happiness of heaven.

17. From whom do we learn to know, love and serve God?

We learn to know, love and serve God
from Jesus Christ, the Son of God,
who teaches us through the Catholic
  Church.

18. How do you know God?

I know God by my faith
in the teaching of the Catholic Church.

19. How do you love God?

I love God by worshiping God at Mass and in my daily prayers.

20. How do you serve God?

I serve God by obeying the commandments of God
and the instructions of the Church.

Jesus said: "If you love me, keep my commandments."

God made all things from nothing

Part Two — CREATION

---

3 GOD THE CREATOR

21. Why is God called the Creator?

God is called the Creator
because he made all things
in heaven and earth from nothing.

22. What do we call all the things God has made?

We call all the things God has made—
his creatures.

23. Which are the chief creatures of God?

The chief creatures of God
are angels and men.

24. What are angels?

Angels are spirits without bodies.

25. Who are the good angels?

The good angels obeyed God
and are now in heaven with him.
They help us to be good.

26. Who are the bad angels?

The bad angels disobeyed God
and are now called devils
who tempt us to sin.

27. Who is your Guardian Angel?

My Guardian Angel is the good angel
God gave me to take care of me
and to lead me to heaven.

28. How do you show your love for your Guardian Angel?

I show my love for my Guardian Angel
by praying to him and listening to him
when he tells me to be good.

29. What is man?

Man is a creature with a body and a soul,
made to the image of God.

30. Why is man made to the image of God?
Man is made to the image of God
because he has a soul,
and, like God, he can know and love.

31. Who were the first man and woman?
The first man and woman were
Adam and Eve.

God made Adam and Eve

32. What great gift did God give Adam and Eve?
God gave Adam and Eve
the great gift of sanctifying grace,
which made them children of God
and gave them the right to heaven.

33. Who made you?
God made me,
with the help of my father and mother.

34. Why did God make you?
God made me to show his goodness
and to make me happy with him
forever in heaven.

35. What must you do to be happy with God in heaven?
To be happy with God in heaven
I must know him, love him,
and serve him in this world.

Our Guardian Angel
helps us to study
our religion

An Angel gave Mary God's message

Part Three — JESUS CHRIST

---

4 JESUS CHRIST, SAVIOR AND REDEEMER OF THE WORLD

36. What does the incarnation mean?

The incarnation means that Jesus Christ,
the Son of God,
the second Person of the Blessed Trinity,
became man
and came to live among us.

37. Why did the Son of God become man?

The Son of God became man
to bring us his own divine life
and to save us from sin.

38. How does Jesus Christ give us his divine life?

Jesus Christ gives us his divine life
through his sanctifying grace,
which makes us holy.

39. When did the Son of God become man?

The Son of God became man
when God sent the angel Gabriel
to ask Mary
to be the Mother of his Son,
and she said "Yes."
Then God sent his Son to her
by the power of his Holy Spirit.

Jesus was born in a stable

40. When was Jesus born?

Jesus was born on the first Christmas Day,
more than nineteen hundred years ago.

41. Is Jesus Christ both God and man?

Jesus Christ is both God and Man—
he is the Son of God and the Son of Mary.

42. Why did the Son of God come to live among us?

The Son of God came to live among us
to make up for the sins of all people
and to help them to gain heaven.

43. What great gift did Jesus come to get back for us?

The great gift
which Jesus came to get back for us
is sanctifying grace,
God's life in us.

44. Why is Jesus called our Redeemer?

Jesus is called our Redeemer
because he paid our debt for sin
and bought heaven back for us
by his suffering and death on the cross,
and by his resurrection from the dead.

45. Why did Jesus suffer and die for us?

Jesus suffered and died for us
because he loved and obeyed his Father,
and because he loved us.

Jesus died because he loved his Father and us

46. What do we mean by the resurrection of Jesus?

By the resurrection of Jesus we mean
that Jesus came back to life again
on Easter Sunday,
three days after he was buried.

Jesus rose from the dead to give us God's life

47. Why did Jesus rise from the dead?

Jesus rose from the dead
to show that he is true God
and to teach us that we, too,
shall rise from the dead,
and in him we are made new persons.

48. When did Jesus return to heaven?

Jesus returned to heaven forty days
after he rose from the dead.

5 THE HOLY SPIRIT IN THE CHURCH

49. Who is the Holy Spirit?
The Holy Spirit is God,
the third Person of the Holy Trinity.

50. What did Jesus tell us about the Holy Spirit?
Jesus told us that the Holy Spirit is God
and that he would send him
from the Father
that he might remain with us.

51. When did the Holy Spirit come to the Church?
The Holy Spirit came to the Church
on Pentecost Sunday,
fifty days after the resurrection of Jesus.

52. What does the Holy Spirit do for us?
The Holy Spirit makes us holy
by giving us his grace.

53. What does the Holy Spirit do for the Church?

The Holy Spirit guides the Church
in the truth
that it may lead people to eternal life.

Jesus sent the Holy Spirit from the Father

St. Peter's basilica in Rome — the center of the Church

Part Five – THE CHURCH

---

6   THE CATHOLIC CHURCH

54. Why did Jesus start the Church?

Jesus started the Church
to bring all people to eternal salvation.

55. What power did Jesus give to his apostles?

Jesus gave his apostles, the first bishops,
the power to teach
and to guide people to God
and help them to be holy.

56. To whom did Jesus give special power in his Church?

Jesus gave special power in his Church
to Saint Peter
by making him the head of the apostles.

57. Who take the place of the apostles today?

The bishops take the place
of the apostles today
as shepherds of the Church.

58. Who help the bishops in the care of people?

The priests help the bishops
in the care of people.

59. Who is the pope?

The pope is the head of the Church,
and takes the place of Jesus on earth.

60. What are the gifts of God in the Catholic Church?

The gifts of God
in the Catholic Church are:
the truths of faith,
and the sacraments.

61. Who guides the Church and gives it life?

Jesus guides the Church
and gives it his own life of grace
through the Holy Spirit,
whom he sent to his Church.

62. How does the Holy Spirit act in the Church?

The Holy Spirit acts in the Church
especially in the sacraments
which Jesus began.

Part Six — THE SACRAMENTS

7   THE SEVEN SACRAMENTS

63. What is a sacrament?

A sacrament is a sign that we can see
made by Christ to give grace.

**64. Why did Jesus give his sacraments
to the Church?**

Jesus gave his sacraments to the Church
to make us holy by his grace,
to build up his Church,
and to give worship to God.

**65. How does the Church want us to receive
the sacraments?**

The Church wants us
to receive the sacraments
often and with faith
that we may receive the grace we need
to live a better Christian life.

66. What are the seven sacraments called?

1 Baptism,
2 Confirmation,
3 Holy Eucharist,
4 Penance,
5 Anointing of the Sick,
6 Holy Orders,
7 and Matrimony.

67. What is baptism?

Baptism is a new birth as a child of God,
the beginning of a new life
of God's grace in us.

68. What did baptism do for you?

Baptism washed away
original sin from my soul,
and gave me sanctifying grace
that was lost for us by Adam.

69. What does the grace of baptism help you to do?

The grace of baptism helps me
to live as a child of God
and to become more like Jesus.

Baptism
Is a
Second Birth

70. What is confirmation?

Confirmation is the sacrament
by which those born again in baptism
receive now the Holy Spirit,
the gift of the Father and the Son.

71. What does Jesus do for you in confirmation?

In confirmation Jesus sends
the Holy Spirit to me again
and gives me new strength
to live a Christian life.

Jesus sends his Holy Spirit to us

72. What is the Anointing of the Sick?

The Anointing of the Sick
is the sacrament
for the seriously ill,
infirm, and aged.

73. What is Holy Orders?

Holy Orders is the sacrament
by which Jesus shares the work
of his priesthood with other men—
the bishops, priests and deacons
of the Catholic Church.

74. What is matrimony?

Matrimony is a sacrament
in which Jesus Christ makes marriage
a lifelong, sacred union of husband
and wife,
by which they give
themselves
to each other
and to him.

Jesus forgives
our sins through
the priest.

8 THE SACRAMENT OF PENANCE

75. What is the sacrament of penance?

The sacrament of penance
brings us God's forgiveness
for the sins we committed after baptism.

76. What does Jesus do for you in the sacrament of penance?

In the sacrament of penance
Jesus comes to forgive my sins
and brings peace with God
and with the Church,
which is hurt by my sins.

77. How do you receive God's forgiveness?

I receive God's forgiveness
through the priest
who has the power to take away sin.

78. Why does the priest have the power to take away sin?

The priest has the power to take away sin
because Jesus gave that power
to his apostles and to his Church
in the Holy Priesthood.

79. Why must you be sorry for your sins before they can be forgiven?

I must be sorry for my sins
before they can be forgiven
because by my sins
I have offended God, my Father,
and because Jesus suffered on the cross
for my sins.

80. What does true sorrow for sin do for you?

True sorrow for sin
brings back the grace of God
if I have lost it by serious (mortal) sin.

81. What must you do if you have committed a serious sin?

If I have committed a serious sin
I must receive the sacrament of penance
before receiving the Holy Eucharist.

82. How does Jesus help you to be holy in the sacrament of penance?

Jesus helps me to be holy
in the sacrament of penance
because he sends his Holy Spirit
to my soul
with grace and strength
to live a better Christian life
and to keep away from sin.

83. What must you do to receive the sacrament of penance?

To receive the sacrament of penance
I must:
1. Find out my sins.
2. Be sorry for my sins.
3. Make up my mind not to sin again.
4. Tell my sins to the priest.
5. Do the penance the priest gives me.

84. How do you find out your sins?

I find out my sins
by remembering the Commandments of
   God,
and asking myself how I have disobeyed
   God.

JESUS CURES A PARALYZED MAN

One day some men brought a sick man to Jesus, and Jesus said to him, "My friend, your sins are forgiven."

Some asked, "Who can forgive sins, but God alone?" Jesus knew their thoughts and said, "That you may know that I have the power to forgive sins, I say to this man, 'Get up. Take your mat with you and return to your house.'"

At once the paralyzed man stood up and walked through the crowd, praising God.

Jesus worked this miracle to show that he could forgive sins because he was God.

Preparation for Confession

Did I commit any of these sins?

The Ten Commandments of God
GOD

1. I, the Lord, am your God, You shall not have other gods besides me.

Did I miss my morning or night prayers?
Did I misbehave during Mass?

HOLY NAME

2. You shall not take the name of the Lord, your God, in vain.

Did I use holy names, like "Jesus" and "God" when I should not have used them?

SUNDAY

3. Remember to keep holy the sabbath day.

Did I miss Mass through my own fault on Sunday or Holy Days?

PARENTS

4. Honor your father and your mother.

Did I disobey my parents or teachers?
Was I mean to them?
Did I answer back?
Did I make fun of my parents or old people?

BE KIND

5. You shall not kill.

Did I hate anyone?

Did I do anything mean to anyone?

Did I let myself get angry?

Did I call anyone bad names?

Did I quarrel and fight?

Did I wish anything bad to anyone?

Did I make anyone sin?

BE PURE

6. You shall not commit adultery.

9. You shall not covet your neighbor's wife

Did I do anything that was really impure?

Was it alone or with others?

Did I willingly keep impure thoughts in my mind?

Did I sin by using impure words?

Did I sin by looking at or reading anything impure?

Did I sin by talking about or listening to anything impure?

BE HONEST

7. You shall not steal.

10. You shall not covet anything that belongs to your neighbor.

Did I steal anything?

Did I keep anything that did not belong to me?

Did I damage what belongs to someone else?

BE TRUTHFUL

8. You shall not bear false witness against your neighbor.

Did I tell any lies?

Did I tell mean things about anyone?

Did I like to listen to unkind talk about others?

A SHORT ACT OF CONTRITION

Lord, I believe in you: increase my faith.

I trust in you: strengthen my trust.

I love you: let me love you more and more.

I am sorry for my sins: deepen my sorrow.

I ask your help: never let me offend you again.

An Act of Contrition explained

O my God, I am heartily sorry
I am really sorry with all my heart.

for having offended You,
I have hurt God by my sins.

and I detest all my sins,
I hate my sins because they hurt God
and Jesus, who died for me.

because of your just punishments,
I do not want to make God punish me
either in this world or in the next.

but most of all, because they offend you,
my God, who are all-good
God never gets tired of being good to me.
He is as good as he can be,
and my sins hurt him.

and deserving of all my love.
God should have all my love
because he loves me.

I firmly resolve,
I really promise to try to keep from sin.

with the help of your grace
When I want to do what is right,
God helps me.
Grace is the name of the help God gives
me.

to sin no more
    I do not want to sin again
and to avoid the near occasions of sin.
    I want to stay away from any persons,
    places, or things that easily get me to sin.

85. How do you make your confession?

I make my confession in this way:
1. I make the sign of the cross.
2. I tell the priest when I made my last confession.
3. I confess my sins.
4. I listen to what the priest tells me.
5. I say the act of contrition.
6. I thank the priest.

86. What do you do after confession?

After confession I say the penance
the priest has given me,
and I thank God for forgiving my sins.

87. How often should you go to confession?

I should go to confession as often as I can
—even every month—
if I really love God
and want to get the grace
to keep away from sin.

At the Last Supper Jesus gave us the Holy Eucharist

9   THE HOLY EUCHARIST

88. What is the Holy Eucharist?

The Holy Eucharist is the sacrament
in which Christ himself,
true God and true Man,
is really present,
offered, and received
in a special sacramental way,
under the appearances of bread and wine.

89. When did Jesus give us the Holy Eucharist?

Jesus gave us the Holy Eucharist
at the Last Supper,
the night before he died.

90. What happened at the Last Supper?

At the Last Supper,
when Jesus said, "This is my body,"
the bread was changed into his body;
and when he said, "This is my blood,"
the wine was changed into his blood.

91. When did Jesus give his priests the power to change bread and wine into his body and blood?

Jesus gave his priests the power
to change bread and wine
into his body and blood
when he said to the apostles
at the Last Supper:
"Do this in memory of me."

92. What happens when a priest speaks the words of consecration at Holy Mass?

When a priest speaks
the words of consecration at Holy Mass,
the bread and wine is changed
into the body and blood of Christ,
given in sacrifice.
It is Jesus who acts through the priest.

93. What does Jesus do in the Mass?

In the Mass Jesus gives himself
to his heavenly Father,
as he did on the cross,
but now in an unbloody manner
in this sacrament,
for he cannot suffer anymore.

94. Why does Jesus give himself to his Father in the Mass?

Jesus gives himself to his Father
in the Mass
to continue the sacrifice of the cross,
to adore and thank his Father,
to ask pardon for our sins,
and to bring his blessing
upon us.

95. What is Holy Communion?

Holy Communion is a holy meal
in which we receive the body and blood
of Jesus Christ
and recall that at the Last Supper
Jesus promised to nourish us
with himself
so that God's life and grace
would be available to us
throughout our lives.

96. Why do you believe that Jesus gives himself to you in Holy Communion?

I believe that Jesus gives himself to me
in Holy Communion because he said,
"This is my body. This is my blood,"
and because the Church teaches
that he is present in this sacrament
as God and Man.

97. What does Holy Communion do for you?

Holy Communion gives me Jesus,
and also the grace I need to love God
and all people,
and to live a holy life as Jesus did.

98. Why does Jesus live in your soul after Holy Communion?

Jesus lives in my soul after Holy Communion
because he promised:
"He who eats my flesh
and drinks my blood,
lives in me and I in him."

99. How can you get ready to receive Holy Communion?

I can get ready to receive Holy Communion
by following the prayers
of the Holy Mass with devotion,
and by saying my own prayers to Jesus.

100. What prayers can you say before Holy Communion?

Before Holy Communion I can tell Jesus
that I believe in him, hope in him,
and love him with all my heart,
and that I am truly sorry for my sins.

101. What prayers can you say after Holy Communion?

After Holy Communion I can
thank Jesus for coming to me,
tell him how much I love him,
and ask him to help me and my family
and all other people.

102. Why should you receive Holy Communion at every Mass?

I should receive Holy Communion
at every Mass
because Holy Communion is a sacrament
—an important part of the Mass—
and because Jesus will give me
the grace I need
to become more like him in my daily life.

St. Michael drove the bad Angels from heaven

Part Seven — THE SINS OF MAN

10 THE FIRST SIN

103. What is sin?
Sin is disobedience to God's laws.

104. What does sin do?
Sin offends God
and brings his punishment upon us
and shows that we do not love him.

105. What happened to the bad angels?
The bad angels disobeyed God
and were cast into hell by the good angels

106. Who committed the first sin on earth?
Adam and Eve, our first parents,
committed the first sin on earth.

107. How did Adam and Eve sin?
Adam and Eve disobeyed God
by eating of the forbidden fruit.

108. What is the sin of Adam and Eve called?
The sin of Adam and Eve is called original
sin,
because it is passed on to us
through our "origin" from Adam.

109. How is original sin passed on to us
Original sin is passed on to us
because we are born
without grace in our souls.

110. What happened to Adam and Eve because of their sin?
Because of their sin
Adam and Eve lost sanctifying grace
and the right to heaven,
and were driven
from the Garden of Paradise.

111. What punishments come to us through original sin?
Through original sin
the punishments of Adam come to us:
we must suffer, fight against evil, and die.

112. What must we have to get to heaven?

To get to heaven we must have
the great gift of God—sanctifying grace.

113. What did God promise?

God promised to send a Savior,
Jesus Christ, his Son,
to make up for the sin of Adam and Eve
and our own sins,
and to get back for us
the gift of sanctifying grace.

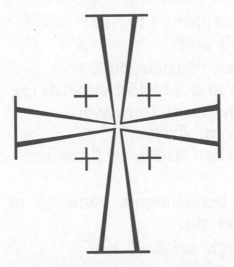

Jesus died for our sins

11 OUR OWN SINS

114. What is actual sin?
Actual sin is any sin
which we ourselves commit.

115. How many kinds of actual sin are there?
There are two kinds of actual sin:
mortal and venial sin.

116. What is mortal sin?
Mortal sin is a serious offense
against the law of God.

117. Why is this sin called mortal?
This sin is called mortal
because it takes away sanctifying grace,
God's life in our soul.

118. When do we commit mortal sin?

We commit mortal sin
when we break a SERIOUS commandment of God,
and KNOW what we are doing,
and WANT to do it.

119. What does mortal sin do to us?

Mortal sin makes us enemies of God
and robs our soul of his sanctifying grace.

120. What is venial sin?

Venial sin is a less serious offense
against the law of God.

121. Does venial sin displease God?

Venial sin displeases God,
weakens our love for God
and shows that we do not love him as we
should.

122. Does venial sin break our friendship with God?

Venial sin does not break our friendship
with God
or rob our souls of his grace.

123. Will God forgive all our sins?

God will forgive all our sins
if we are truly sorry for them
and try to keep from committing them
again.

Jesus gives us grace
through the Holy Spirit

Part Eight — THE LIFE OF GRACE

12 THE NEW LIFE IN THE SPIRIT

124. What is sanctifying grace?
Sanctifying grace is a gift of God
by which our soul shares
in the very life of God.

125. How do we share in God's own life?
We share in God's own life
by faith, hope, and love.

126. What is faith?
Faith is a gift of God
by which the Holy Spirit helps us
to accept God's word and to give
ourselves to the heavenly Father.

127. What is hope?

Hope is a gift of God
which helps us to know
that God loves us and cares for us,
and that we can trust in him.

128. What is love?

Love is a gift of God
which helps us to love God,
and to love all people for the love of God
because they too belong to him.

129. What does grace do for us?

Through grace the Holy Spirit
makes us holy and pleasing to God
and helps us to live as children of God.

130. Is grace also God's gift of himself?

Grace is also God's gift of himself
because the Holy Spirit unites us with
   God by love
and lives in our soul as in a temple.

131. How long does sanctifying grace stay in our soul?

Sanctifying grace stays in our soul
as long as we do not lose it
by committing a mortal sin.

132. What other kind of grace does the Holy Spirit give us?

The Holy Spirit also gives us actual grace.

133. What does actual grace do for us?

Actual grace gives light to our mind,
and strength to our will
to do good and to avoid evil.

134. How can you keep from committing sin?

I can keep from committing sin:
1. by praying,
2. by receiving the sacraments often,
3. by remembering that God
   is always with me
   and that I am a temple of the Holy
      Spirit,
4. by keeping busy with work and play,
5. by fighting temptation at once,
6. by staying away from whatever might
   lead me to sin.

135. What has God willed for our salvation?

God has willed
that we live in his sanctifying grace
as his children,
and that we reach eternal life with him.

We love God when we obey his commandments

Part Nine — THE MORAL LIFE

---

13 THE TEN COMMANDMENTS OF GOD

136. What must we do to show that we love God?

To show that we love God
we must obey everything that Jesus has
    commanded,
and believe all that he has taught.

137. What is the greatest commandment of God?

The greatest commandment of God is
to love him with all our heart
and all people for his sake.

138. What are we commanded by the first com mandment of God?

The first commandment is:
I, the Lord, am your God.
You shall not have other gods besides me.
We must not put anyone or anything
in place of God.

139. What are we commanded by the second commandment?

The second commandment is:
You shall not take the name of the Lord,
your God, in vain.
We must always speak with reverence
of God and the saints.

140. What are we commanded by the third commandment?

The third commandment is:
Remember to keep holy the sabbath day.
We must worship God on Sunday
by assisting at the Holy Sacrifice of the
Mass.

141. What are we commanded by the fourth commandment?

The fourth commandment is:
Honor your father and your mother.
We must love and obey our parents.

142. What are we commanded by the fifth commandment?

The fifth commandment is:
You shall not kill.
We must take good care of our health and help others to do the same.

143. What are we commanded by the sixth commandment?

The sixth commandment is:
You shall not commit adultery.
We must be pure in our words and actions.

144. What are we commanded by the seventh commandment?

The seventh commandment is:
You shall not steal.
We must respect what belongs to others.

145. What are we commanded by the eighth commandment?

The eighth commandment is:
You shall not bear false witness against your neighbor.
We must speak the truth in all things.

146. What are we commanded by the ninth commandment?

The ninth commandment is:
You shall not covet your neighbor's wife.
We must be pure in thought and in desire.

147. What are we commanded by the tenth commandment?

The tenth commandment is:
You shall not covet anything
that belongs to your neighbor.
We must not want to take or to keep
what belongs to others.

Jesus said, "If you love me, keep my commandments."

Jesus makes Mary our Mother and Queen

14 MARY THE MOTHER OF GOD AND THE CHURCH

148. Why should we honor the Blessed Virgin Mary?

We should honor the Blessed Virgin Mary
by showing her our love and devotion
as the Mother of Jesus Christ,
and the Mother of the Church,
for she is our spiritual Mother.

149. What special gifts did Mary receive from God?

The special gifts Mary received
from God are these:
she is the Mother of God,
she was kept free from original sin,
she was taken body and soul to heaven.

The Holy Family is the patron of families

150. Why does the Church honor the saints?
The Church honors the saints
because they help us by their prayers
and by the good example of their lives.

151. What must we do for those who have died?
We must honor the bodies of those
who have died
and pray for their souls.

Jesus said we must become like children to reach heaven

Part Eleven — UNION WITH GOD IN HEAVEN

15 JUDGMENT, PURGATORY, HELL, HEAVEN

152. What should we look forward to during this life?

During this life we should look forward to our reunion with God.

153. What is the particular judgment?

The particular judgment is the judgment which will be passed on each one of us after death.

154. What happens in purgatory?

In purgatory our soul is made clean before we are able to see God.

56

155. What will happen at the last judgment?

At the last judgment
all of us will stand
before the judgment seat of Christ
so that each one may receive
what he deserves,
according to what he has done on earth,
good or evil.

156. What will happen to those who have done evil?

Those who have done evil
will rise from the dead
and will be punished in hell forever.

157. What will happen to those who have done good?

Those who have done good
will rise to live an eternal life with God
and will receive the reward
of seeing him in unending joy.

158. What should we do during our life on earth?

During our life on earth
we should love and serve God faithfully
so that we may be ready for our death
and our resurrection with Christ
to eternal life in heaven.

THE TEN COMMANDMENTS OF GOD

1. I, the Lord, am your God. You shall not have other gods besides me.
2. You shall not take the name of the Lord, your God, in vain.
3. Remember to keep holy the sabbath day.
4. Honor your father and your mother.
5. You shall not kill.
6. You shall not commit adultery.
7. You shall not steal.
8. You shall not bear false witness against your neighbor.
9. You shall not covet your neighbor's wife.
10. You shall not covet anything that belongs to your neighbor.

In the Sermon on the Mount Jesus spoke of the Beatitudes.

THE BEATITUDES

1. Blest are the poor in spirit:
   the reign of God is theirs.
2. Blest are the sorrowing:
   they shall be consoled.
3. Blest are the lowly:
   they shall inherit the land.
4. Blest are they who hunger and thirst
   for holiness: they shall have their fill.
5. Blest are they who show mercy:
   mercy shall be theirs.
6. Blest are the single-hearted:
   for they shall see God.
7. Blest are the peacemakers:
   they shall be called sons of God.
8. Blest are those persecuted for holiness' sake:
   the reign of God is theirs. *(Mt 5:3-10)*

DUTIES OF CATHOLICS
Chief Precepts of the Church

1. To keep holy the day of the Lord's Resurrection: to worship God by participating in Mass every Sunday and holy day of obligation: to avoid those activities that would hinder renewal of soul and body, e.g., needless work and business activities, unnecessary shopping and so on.

2. To lead a sacramental life: to receive Holy Communion frequently and the Sacrament of Penance — minimally, to receive the Sacrament of Penance at least once a year (annual confession is obligatory only if serious sin is involved).

— Minimally also, to receive Holy Communion at least once a year, between the First Sunday of Lent and Trinity Sunday.

3. To study Catholic teaching in preparation for the Sacrament of Confirmation, to be confirmed, and then to continue to study and advance the cause of Christ.

4. To observe the marriage laws of the Church: to give religious training, by example and word, to one's children; to use parish schools and catechetical programs.

5. To strengthen and support the Church: one's own parish community and parish priests, the world-wide Church and the Pope.

6. To do penance, including abstaining from meat and fasting from food on the appointed days.

7. To join in the missionary spirit and apostolate of the Church.

APPENDIX B — GENERAL PRAYERS
Recommended by the National Conference of Catholic Bishops

SIGN OF THE CROSS

IN the name of the Father, and of the Son,
and of the Holy Spirit. Amen.

THE LORD'S PRAYER

OUR Father, who art in heaven,
hallowed be Thy name;
Thy kingdom come,
Thy will be done
on earth as it is in heaven.
Give us this day our daily bread,
and forgive us our trespasses,
as we forgive those who trespass against us;
and lead us not into temptation,
but deliver us from evil. Amen.

HAIL MARY

HAIL Mary, full of grace!
the Lord is with thee;
blessed art thou among women,
and blessed is the fruit of thy womb, Jesus.
Holy Mary, Mother of God,
pray for us sinners,
now and at the hour of our death. Amen.

GLORY BE

GLORY be to the Father,
and to the Son,
and to the Holy Spirit,
as it was in the beginning,
is now, and ever shall be,
world without end. Amen.

THE APOSTLES' CREED

I BELIEVE in God,
the Father Almighty,
Creator of heaven and earth,
and in Jesus Christ, His only Son, our Lord,
who was conceived by the Holy Spirit,
born of the Virgin Mary,
suffered under Pontius Pilate,
was crucified, died and was buried;
he descended into hell;
on the third day he rose again from the dead;
he ascended into heaven,
and is seated at the right hand of God the Father
Almighty;
from there he will come to judge the living and the
dead.

I believe in the Holy Spirit,
the holy Catholic Church,
the Communion of Saints,
the forgiveness of sins,
the resurrection of the body,
and life everlasting. Amen.

ACT OF FAITH

O MY God,
I firmly believe all the truths
that the holy Catholic Church believes and
teaches.
I believe these truths, O Lord,
because You, the infallible Truth,
have revealed them to her;
in this faith I am resolved to live and die.

ACT OF HOPE

O MY God, trusting in Your promises,
and because You are faithful,
powerful and merciful,
I hope, through the merits of Jesus Christ,
for the pardon of my sins,
final perseverance,
and the blessed glory of heaven.

ACT OF LOVE

O MY God,
because You are infinite Goodness
and worthy of infinite love,
I love You
with my whole heart above all things,
and for love of You,
I love my fellowmen as myself.

ACT OF CONTRITION

O MY God,
I am heartily sorry for having offended You,
and I detest all my sins,
because of Your just punishments,
but most of all because they offend You,
my God,
who are all good and deserving of all my love.
I firmly resolve,
with the help of Your grace, to sin no more
and to avoid the near occasions of sin.

ACT OF CONSECRATION

L ORD Jesus Christ,
take all my freedom,
my memory, my understanding,
and my will.
All that I have and cherish
you have given me.
Give me these, Lord Jesus,
and I ask for nothing more.

THE MYSTERIES OF THE ROSARY
The Joyful Mysteries

1. The Annunciation of the Archangel Gabriel to the Virgin Mary.
2. The Visitation of the Virgin Mary.
3. The Birth of Our Lord at Bethlehem.
4. The Presentation of Our Lord in the Temple.
5. The Finding of Our Lord in the Temple.

The Luminous Mysteries

1. The Baptism of Jesus in the Jordan.
2. Christ's Self-Manifestation at Cana.
3. Christ's Proclamation of God's Kingdom.
4. The Transfiguration of the Lord.
5. Christ's Institution of the Eucharist.

The Sorrowful Mysteries

1. The Agony of Our Lord in the Garden of Gethsemane.
2. The Scourging of Our Lord at the Pillar.
3. The Crowning of Our Lord with Thorns.
4. The Carrying of the Cross by Our Lord to Calvary.
5. The Crucifixion and Death of Our Lord.

The Glorious Mysteries

1. The Resurrection of Our Lord from the Dead.
2. The Ascension of Our Lord into Heaven.
3. The Descent of the Holy Spirit upon the Apostles.
4. The Assumption of Mary into Heaven.
5. The Coronation of Mary as Queen of Heaven and Earth.

HAIL, HOLY QUEEN

HAIL, holy Queen, Mother of mercy; hail our life, our sweetness, and our hope. To you do we cry, poor banished children of Eve. To you do we send up our sighs, mourning and weeping in this valley of tears. Turn then, most gracious Advocate, your eyes of mercy toward us. And after this our exile show to us the blessed fruit of your womb, Jesus, O clement, O loving, O sweet Virgin Mary.

THE ANGELUS

THE Angel of the Lord declared to Mary.
And she conceived by the Holy Spirit.
Hail Mary . . . .
Behold the handmaid of the Lord.
Be it done to me according to your word.
Hail Mary . . . .
And the Word was made flesh.
And dwelt among us.
Hail Mary . . . .
Pray for us, O holy Mother of God.
That we may be made worthy of the promises of Christ.

Let us pray
Pour forth, we beseech You, O Lord, your grace into our hearts; that as we have known the incarnation of Christ, your Son, by the message of the angel, so, by his Passion and Cross, we may be brought to the glory of his resurrection. Through the same Christ our Lord. Amen.

GRACE BEFORE MEALS

BLESS us, O Lord, and these Your gifts which we are about to receive from Your bounty. Through Christ our Lord. Amen.

GRACE AFTER MEALS

WE give You thanks, Almighty God, for all Your benefits, who live and reign world without end. Amen.

MY DAILY PRAYER

MY God,
I believe in You,
the one true God.
I believe that in You
there are three Divine Persons —
God the Father,
God the Son,
and God the Holy Spirit.

Make me strong in my faith.
Son of God,
I believe that for love of us
You became Man,
without ceasing to be God.

I believe that You are my Lord
and my Savior Jesus Christ,
the Redeemer of the human race,
who died on the cross
for the salvation of all men,
who died also for me.

PRAYERS BEFORE HOLY COMMUNION

JESUS, I believe in You, Jesus,
I hope in You.

Jesus, I love You with all my heart.

Jesus, I want so much to receive You
into my heart.

I long for You.

Jesus, I am sorry for all my sins.

I am not good enough for You to come to me.

But I know You want me to come to You
that You may make me good.

Jesus, give me Your grace
that I may always please You.

Holy Mary, my dearest Mother,
pray for me
and make my heart ready for Jesus.

Be with me when he comes.

Love him for me.

Good Saint Joseph,
pray for me
that I may love Jesus as you loved him.

My Guardian Angel,
help me to be as good as I can.

Make me a good friend of Jesus.

Jesus, come to me because I love You.

PRAYERS AFTER HOLY COMMUNION

Jesus, I believe in You.
Jesus, I hope in You.
Jesus, I love You with all my heart.
Jesus I thank You for having come to me.
Welcome to my heart and bless me.

You are the same Jesus
Who was born in the stable of Bethlehem.

You are the same Jesus
Who loved Mary and Joseph
and helped them all You could.

You are the same Jesus
Who loved little children
and let them come to You.

You are the same Jesus
Who gave Holy Communion to the Apostles
at the Last Supper.

You are the same Jesus
Who gave Your life for us on the cross
and rose from the dead.

And now You have come to me.
Jesus, I thank You for your love for me.

And now that You are so close to me,
I ask You to help me
to love You more
and to serve You as You want me
to serve You.

Teach me to know You better
and to help other people to love You.

Jesus,
I ask You to help my mother and father,
my brothers and sisters,
our priests and teachers, and everyone.

Help the poor souls in purgatory,
and take them to heaven.

Holy Mary,
you are the Mother of Jesus and my mother.

You so often held him in your arms.
He is now in my heart.

Be with me while He is here.
Adore Him, love Him, and thank Him for me.

Mother Mary,
please help me to be good.
Make me a true friend of Jesus.

Help me to pray often,
and to be obedient,
kind, honest, and truthful.

Keep me from all sin
and help me to come to heaven,
where I will see Jesus and you forever.

HOLY DAYS OF OBLIGATION

THE IMMACULATE CONCEPTION-December 8

This feast reminds us how holy Mary's body and soul were made by God.

THE ASCENSION (40 days after Easter)

The day Our Lord went up to heaven.

CHRISTMAS-December 25

This is Our Lord's birthday.

ASSUMPTION – August 15

The day Our Lady was taken up to heaven.

OCTAVE DAY OF CHRISTMAS – January 1

The day when Our Lord received His name Jesus.

ALL SAINTS – November 1

The day we think of all the saints in heaven.

BASIC ANSWERS

FIll in the Blanks

The numeral at the end of each sentence shows which question gives the answer. These answers should be written out on a separate sheet of paper as homework or they can be discussed with the class.

Chapter 1. The Holy Trinity

1. God made himself known to us through .... (3)
2. Jesus taught us that in the one God there are .... (6)
3. Jesus taught us to love our heavenly Father because .... (8)
4. Jesus taught us that he is .... (9)
5. Jesus taught us that the Holy Spirit is .... (10)

Chapter 2. Worship of God

6. God has shown his love for us by .... (12)
7. We worship God by .... (14)
8. We worship God especially in Holy Mass because .... (15)
9. God put us in this world to .... (16)
10. We learn to know, love and serve God from . (17)
11. I know God by .... (18)
12. I love God by .... (19)
13. I serve God by .... (20)

Chapter 3. God the Creator

14. God is called the Creator because .... (21)
15. Angels are .... (24)
16. My Guardian Angel is .... (27)
17. Man is .... (29)

41. The bishops take the place of .... (57)
42. The pope is .... (59)
43. The gifts of God in the Catholic Church are:
.... (60)
44. Jesus guides the Church and gives it his own life of grace through .... (61)
45. The Holy Spirit acts in the Church especially in .... (62)

Chapter 7. The Seven Sacraments

46. A sacrament is .... (63)
47. Jesus gave his sacraments to the Church to .... (64)
48. The Church wants us to receive the sacraments often and with faith that .... (65)
49. The seven sacraments are called .... (66)
50. Baptism is a .... (67)
51. Baptism washed away .... and gave me .... (68)
52. The grace of baptism helps me to .... (69)
53. Confirmation is .... (70)
54. In confirmation Jesus .... (71)
55. The Anointing of the Sick is .... (72)
56. Holy Orders is .... (73)
57. Matrimony is .... (74)

Chapter 8. The Sacrament of Penance

58. The sacrament of penance brings us .... (75)
59. In the sacrament of penance Jesus comes to .... (76)
60. The priest has the power to take away sin because .... (78)
61. I must be sorry for my sins before they can be forgiven because .... (79)

62. True sorrow for sin brings back .... (80)
63. If I have committed a serious sin I must ...... (81)
64. Jesus helps me to be holy in the sacrament of penance because .... (82)
65. To receive the sacrament of penance I must .... (83)
66. I find out my sins by .... (84)
67. I make my confession in this way: .... (85)

Chapter 9. The Holy Eucharist

68. The Holy Eucharist is .... (88)
69. At the Last Supper, when Jesus said, "This is my body," the bread .... and when he said: "This is my blood," the wine .... (90)
70. Jesus gave his priests the power to change bread and wine into his body and blood when .... (91)
71. When a priest speaks the words of consecration at Holy Mass, the bread and wine are changed into .... (92)
72. In the Mass Jesus gives himself to .... (93)
73. Jesus gives himself to his Father in the Mass to .... (94)
74. Holy Communion is .... (95)
75. I believe that Jesus gives himself to me in Holy Communion because .... (96)
76. Holy Communion gives me .... (97)
77. Jesus lives in my soul after Holy Communion because .... (98)
78. Before Holy Communion I can tell Jesus that .... (100)

79. After Holy Communion I can thank Jesus for ....
.... and tell him................. and ask him
to .... (101)
80. We should receive Holy Communion at every
Mass because .... (102)

10. The First Sin

81. Sin is .... (103)
82. Sin .... God and brings .... (104)
83. Adam and Eve disobeyed God by .... (107)
84. The sin of Adam and Eve is called original sin,
because .... (108)
85. Original sin is passed on to us because ...... (109)
86. Because of their sin Adam and Eve lost ...... (110)
87. Through original sin the punishments of Adam come
to us: we must .... (111)
88. To get to heaven we must .... (112)
89. God promised to send a Savior, Jesus Christ, his
Son to .... (113)

Chapter 11. Our Own Sins

90. Actual sin is .... (114)
91. Mortal sin is .... (116)
92. This sin is called mortal because .... (117)
93. We commit mortal sin when .... (118)
94. Mortal sin makes us .... and robs our soul of
.... (119)
95. Venial sin displeases .... weakens .... and
shows that .... (121)
96. Venial sin .... our friendship with God (122)
97. God will forgive all our sins if .... (123)

Chapter 12.　The New Life in the Spirit

Chapter 13.　The Ten Commandments of God

Chapter 14

Mary the Mother of God and the Church

Chapter 15. Judgment, Purgatory, Hell, Heaven

NOTE TO PARENTS

DEAR parents and teachers, you are privileged to be able to prepare a child of God for first Confession and Communion. At no time in their lives are these children more open to accept the seeds of divine truth which you will give them. So much of their future spiritual life will depend on the way you prepare them for these two important sacraments, because these sacraments can be received frequently in their life-time. You share in the priestly work of Christ the Teacher, and through the Sacrament of Confirmation you have the opportunity to be a witness to Jesus Christ by implanting his truth in the hearts of the children whom he loved so dearly. May this catechism be a worthy instrument to help you do your apostolic work well!

The material of this First Communion Catechism follows the Principal Elements of the Christian Message for Catechesis (Ch. V) and Catechesis for a Worshipping Community (Ch. VI) of *Sharing the Light of Faith* — The National Catechetical Directory for Catholics of the United States, approved Oct. 30, 1978. This is also the source of material I have used in the Primary, Intermediate, and Complete Edition of the St. Joseph *New American Catechism.*

The National Catechetical Directory makes some significant comments on Catechesis for the Sacrament of Reconciliation and First Communion.

"Parents have a right and duty to be intimately involved in preparing their children for First Communion. Catechesis aims to help parents grow in understanding and appreciation of the Eucharist and participate readily in catechizing their children.

"Catechesis for children seeks to strengthen their awareness of the Father's love, of the call to participate in Christ's sacrifice, and of the gift of the Spirit. Children should be taught that the Holy Eucharist is the real body and blood of Christ, and what appear to be bread and wine are actually His living body.

78

Children around the age of 7 tend to think concretely; they grasp oonoopto likc 'unity' and 'belonging' from experiences, such as sharing, listening, eating, conversing, giving, thanking, and celebrating. Such experiences, coupled with further efforts to familiarize them with the main events of Jesus' life, help them to participate more meaningfully in the action of the Mass and to receive Christ's body and blood in communion in an informed and reverent manner."(122)

"Catechesis of children for Reconciliation must always respect the natural disposition, ability, age, and circumstances of individuals. It seeks, first, to make clear the relationship of the sacrament to the child's life: second, to help the child recognize moral good and evil, repent of wrongdoing, and turn for forgiveness to Christ and the Church; third, to encourage the child to see that, in this sacrament, faith is expressed by being forgiven and forgiving; fourth, to encourage the child to approach the sacrament freely and regularly. Parents should be involved in the preparation of children for this sacrament.

"Catechesis for the Sacrament of Reconciliation is to precede First Communion and must be kept distinct by a clear and unhurried separation. This is to be done so that the specific identity of each sacrament is apparent and so that, before receiving First Communion, the child will be familiar with the revised Rite of Reconciliation and will be at ease with the reception of the sacrament. The Sacrament of Reconciliation normally should be celebrated prior to the reception of First Communion.

"Because continuing, lifelong conversion is part of what it means to grow in faith, catechesis for the Sacrament of Reconciliation is ongoing. Children have a right to a fuller catechesis each year. Lent is an especially appropriate season for this." (126)

Pope John Paul II in his major document *(Catechesi Tradendae)* discussing catechetical renewal, released Oct. 25, 1979, states:

"Catechesis is an education of children, young people and adults in the faith, which includes especially the teaching of Christian doctrine imparted, generally speaking, in an *organic and systematic way,* with a view to initiating the hearers into the fullness of Christian life.

"Catechetical work must be systematic, not improvised but programmed to reach a precise goal. *It must deal with essentials. . . .* It must be an *integral* Christian initiation, open to all the other factors of Christian life."

In the spirit of the instruction of Pope John Paul II, I have prepared this *St. Joseph New American Catechism Series,* a part of which is this First Communion Catechism. It is a systematic summary of the essentials of Christian Doctrine. A child preparing for First Communion should be put in touch with these essentials at least in a general way in order to be better prepared to receive the Sacrament of Reconciliation and the Most Blessed Sacrament of the Altar.

To make this instruction more effective, I recommend to parents and teachers the frequent use of pictures and stories, especially from the Bible. They will find abundant material especially in two of my publications: *Catechism Sketched,* and *Catechism in Stories,*

Father Lawrence G. Lovasik, S.V.D.